The Visible, Invisible Beginnings. This child's journey; A series of events

Margie M. Garris

AuthorHouse™ LLC
1663 Liberty Drive
Bloomington, IN 47403
www.authorhouse.com
Phone: 1-800-839-8640

Published by AuthorHouse 5/30/2014

ISBN: 978-1-4969-1493-4 (sc)
ISBN: 978-1-4969-1492-7 (e)

Library of Congress Control Number: 2014909405

This book is printed on acid-free paper.

authorHOUSE®

Contents

Preface

Genesis 37:19, (ESV).They said to one another, "Here comes this dreamer.

A portion of the title of this book was taken from an African book cover's title, to which reference girls and young women difficulties. And in so much as a matter of fact how those that were obligated as care givers turn a blind eye toward those same girls and women's circumstances.

(Job 12:22, ESV) He will uncover the deeps of darkness then bring darkness to light

The purpose of this book's writings are to inform, and to place within the universe "circumstances" of hurt, so that those whom were "hurt" could find peace and allow God of all creation to take control within one's life.

Where silence is the benediction for some God disperses HIS angels because there are in some; AFFLICTIONS, the soul sits dumb!

Interpretations

Incest is sexual contact between persons who are so closely related that their marriage is illegal (e.g., parents and children, uncles/aunts and nieces/nephews, etc.). This usually takes the form of an older family member sexually abusing a child or adolescent. (Department of Health and Human Services, 2005)

Incest is especially damaging because it disrupts the child's primary support system, the family.

- o When a child is abused by someone outside the family, the child's family is often able to offer support and a sense of safety.

- o When the abuser is someone in the family, the family may not be able to provide support or a sense of safety. Since the children (especially younger children) often have limited resources outside the family, it can be very hard for them to recover from incest

Incest can damage a child's ability to trust, since the people who were supposed to protect and care for them have abused them.

- o Survivors of incest sometimes have difficulty developing trusting relationships

It can also be very damaging for a child if a non-abusing parent is aware of the abuse and chooses—for whatever reason—not to take action to stop it.

There are many reasons that a non-abusing parent might not stop the abuse.

o The non-abusing parent may feel that they are dependent on the abuser for shelter or income.

o If the non-abusing parent was the victim of incest as a child, they may think that this is normal for families.

o The non-abusing parent may feel that allowing the incest to continue is the only way to keep their partner.

o The non-abusing parent may feel that their child was "asking for it" by behaving in ways that the parent perceives as provocative or seductive.

o Unfortunately, many non-abusing parents are aware of the incest and choose not to get their child out of the situation, or worse, to blame their child for what has happened. This makes the long-term effects of incest worse.

Child Sexual Abuse is sexual abuse that includes sexual intercourse or its deviations. Yet all offences that involve sexually touching a child, as well as non-touching offenses and sexual exploitation, are just as harmful and devastating to a child's well-being. (Bottoms & Epstein, 1998)

Touching sexual offenses include:

- o Fondling;

- o Making a child touch an adult's sexual organs

- o Penetrating a child's vagina or anus no matter how slight with a penis or any object that doesn't have a valid medical purpose.

Sexual abuse is unwanted sexual activity, with perpetrators using force, making threats or taking advantage of victims not able to give consent. Most victims and perpetrators know each other. Immediate reactions to sexual abuse include shock, fear or disbelief. Long-term symptoms include anxiety, fear or post-traumatic stress disorder. While efforts to treat sex offenders remain unpromising, psychological interventions for survivors — especially group therapy — appears effective. (Besharov, 1994)

The invisible girl journey begins here:

◯ ◯ ◯ ◯ ◯
At The Birthday Party

It is dark, short of gloomy and cloudy, a group of invisible girls gathering around a large woman sitting in an armchair next to the door. The group of invisible girls covered the woman's appearance and body, her identity is not known. One of the invisible girls in the group is the invisible girl.

"Let's blow out the candles," one other invisible girl said to me. "Alright", but each child at the birthday party came together and blew at the candles together. The group of invisible girls ran around the house and began playing. Running, dancing, jumping on grown folks laps, laughing, and gee, having lots of fun and enjoying all of it as were the other invisible girls of the group.

Suddenly, someone came to one of the invisible girls and said. "Let's go" A grown up remarked out aloud. She has to go now. The invisible girl began to cry and say. "Let me stay, I don't want to go", says the invisible girl and began crying, hollering and screaming. The invisible girl desired to stay. The grown up woman said, "Awe, she has to go, so sorry, but she has to leave". A huge argument arose among all the grown up women of the house. The grown up woman complexion was dark and their continence was sad.

A large woman placed the invisible girl in the back of her car. A car that was fast and brown. Before, the large woman and the invisible girl drove off. The large woman turned and said to the invisible girl, while pointing one large finger at her." You better be nice to these folks and their children; Do you hear me"; and remember your name is" blank the blank" And, "let me hear you say your name". The invisible girl nodded and said the name not knowing how to sound out all the syllables in the name. The large woman drove on in her fancy looking car.

We drove up to the folk's house, the one with the children in it. The house was large on the east side of the city, three stories high. The house had three floors. The large woman got out of the car. She said to man who was looking out the window holding a baby. "Where is your woman"? The man replied," she is down the street in the projects at a woman house with a lot of children." "Well", said, the large woman. "Hear she is", pointing to the invisible girl and" here is her certificate of birth" The man sitting in the window holding a toddler, looked down at the certificate in his hands and looked down at it The large woman left the invisible girl with the man sitting in the window holding a toddler The large woman got in her fancy car and drove off. The invisible girl was left alone without the large woman in the fancy car. The large woman that had came to the house had drove away.

(Genesis 37:20, ESV) Come now, let us kill him and throw him into one of the pits. [a] Then we will say that a fierce animal has devoured him, and we will see what will become of his dreams."

(Genesis 37:24, ESV) and they took him and threw him into a pit. The pit was empty; there was no water in it.

Lasciviousness is a gross form of wickedness that has sexual overtones in many cases. It starts in a sinful heart (Mark 7:21-22, ESV), and manifests itself in fleshly (carnal) actions (Galatians 5:19), and can lead to a state of being "past feeling" (Ephesians 4:19, ESV).

○ ○ ○ ○ ○
The Vestibule

The large house has three floors First, second and third floor. One night the invisible girl stayed outside playing. The outside grew dark, so the invisible girl came inside. She first had to step into the vestibule of the entrance of the house to get inside of the house. Inside the vestibule, a nearly tall brown boy, was kissing on a not so tall girl. "Hello", said the invisible girl as she interrupted the nearly tall brown boy and the not so tall girl. They abruptly said, "What are you doing here get inside." The invisible girl tried to explain to the boy and girl that she was now their sister. But the boy and girl did not want to hear what she had to say. The invisible girl began to talk again and said, "The large woman in the fancy car told me to be nice to you". The invisible girl ran inside the house and turned around to see if the nearly tall brown boy and the not so tall girl were coming inside the house too. And saw them with their faces close together heads moving together and arms wrapped tightly around one another. Oh, now I realized that the tall brown boy and the not so tall girl are brother and sister.

The lascivious person will not be able to enter the kingdom of heaven (Galatians 5:19-21, ESV). To ignore the biblical warnings is the epitome of folly.

(Ecclesiastics 9:11, ESV)   I have seen something else under the sun: The race is not to the swift or the battle to the strong, nor does food come to the wise or wealth to the brilliant or favor to the learned; but time and chance happen to them all

○ ○ ○ ○ ○
First Day of School

This was the first day of school. The invisible girl is a kindergarten child. The woman that lived in the three story house said to the invisible girl one morning. You are going to school. The invisible girl asked the woman living in the three story house, "Will you take me to school?" The woman living in the three story house, gave the invisible girl a bag lunch, a small notebook, and showed the invisible girl the entrance way out of the three story house. The woman gave the invisible girl directions to the school. The school was 2 -3 blocks from the three story house. The woman pointed the directions toward the school with her finger. The woman told the invisible girl, "Keep walking straight ahead, do not go right or left, keep walking straight; the large red building will be in front of you; that will be your school".

The invisible girl began her journey, she walked and walked and walked, until she came face to face with the large red building. The invisible girl went inside and told the lady at the desk, that this was her first day of school and she is in the kindergarten. The woman at the desk ask the invisible girl her name, and then directed her to her class. While at school during recess, the invisible girl played with other boys and girls. One activity was ring around the rosy, the invisible girl did not like holding hands with one particular little boy who was pale white. The little boy hands was sweaty, and the invisible girl hands began to become sweaty and nervous all at the same time. The invisible girl let go.

After school, the invisible girl walked home. It was a long walk home. The woman living in the three story house was angry at the invisible girl because she had taken a long time to walk home. The woman informed the invisible girl that the not so tall girl will walk with her to school the next day. The woman wanted to know why the invisible girl had taken so much time in walking home from school. The next day the not so tall girl walked with the invisible girl to school, the not so tall girl was walking faster than the invisible girl. The not so tall girl said "You better walk faster or I will leave you". The invisible girl tried with all her might with her little legs to keep in step with the not so tall girl. The invisible little girl, she could not. Therefore, the invisible girl was left behind. The invisible girl walked home alone after school. When she got to the three story house the woman said, "You better walk faster, I want you to be home sooner". The not so tall girl that was with the tall brown boy in the vestibule had told the woman the reason for the invisible girl not making it home sooner. The invisible girl was a slow walker.

○ ○ ○ ○ ○
Outside

One evening it was a late Halloween evening while just about everyone was asleep. The invisible girl was playing outside the house. This was one hot evening and I found out early that most people doing warm weather stayed up late and usually sit outside late. There were some people in the three story house that were not asleep. There were some sitting downstairs on the first floor of the house watching television and talking among one another. These were called grown folks.

The invisible girl was playing outside. It was dark outside, in front of the house. There was not much street lighting and the moon seemed as if it was not shining as bright that evening. It was really late that evening near midnight or maybe just around eleven o'clock. The invisible girl was the only child and person outside that night on that street where she lived in the house with the three floors. She did not get to meet all the siblings in that family; so far all she can remember is the toddler that the man sitting by window was holding and the boy and girl in the vestibule of the house kissing.

Then suddenly one of the grown folks came to the door and asked the invisible girl what she was doing outside. The invisible girl replied that she was playing outside. And the grown folk told her to stay near the house and not to go far from the house. The grown folk went back into the house and the door of the house was left open a little. The invisible girl continued to play.

Suddenly, it became as if a fog had came over the night. The invisible girl felt a little light head then everything cleared up. Suddenly when the fog was removed; there were three small green images, midgets and all green. The invisible girl thinking that these were leprechauns or small green people. The invisible girl speaks to the green leprechauns saying "hello", and waving her hand in a gesture of hello to them. The green leprechauns just stared at her and as quickly as they came after the fog, they quickly left. The invisible girl ran into the house to tell the grown folks what she saw and they laughed. The grown folks went outside to look around and told the invisible girl to come inside. The invisible girl came inside but the next evening around the same time the invisible girl looked for the green leprechauns.   And, again hoping that they would appear; neither the fog nor the little green midgets appeared. The invisible girl became sad. The invisible girl was thinking she had made friends with three little green midgets that were leprechauns. And this was the first Halloween the invisible girl ever encountered.

○ ○ ○ ○ ○
Respite

Having one to spend each day the color of the leaves.

It seems you blend in with so many other ordinary things.

It could make you wonder why, but why wonder why?

And I think it's what I want to be

○ ○ ○ ○ ○
Sleeping In Bed

The makeshift bed that the invisible girl was sleeping on was not a mattress, but a large mattress placed on the floor. Lying, on a mattress, that was a makeshift bed, next to three other children. It was dark in the room. The bed was overcrowded with the other children of the three story house. The invisible girl could not sleep. There was no blankets to cover the bodies of those that were lying on the mattress. A sheet was used as a blanket. The invisible girl pulled the sheet over her face and over her head to sleep. But the light from the hall was shinning into the room. The only light was the light that shined through the bedroom from the hall near where the invisible girl was sleeping. The invisible girl could not sleep. She heard noises in the house. She heard noises in the hallway. The sheet that the invisible girl covered herself with had blanket holes in it. The invisible girl pulled the sheet around to the holes. The invisible girl peered through the hole in the sheet. The invisible girl seen the man that was sitting next to the window that was holding the toddler. The man was looking down toward the mattress. The man began to touch around on the mattress. The invisible girl was afraid and wondered why was the man touching around on the mattress. The man began to call out some names of the children that lived in the three story house, there was no response. The man walked out of the room. This was the beginning of the man that was touching around on the mattress loss of eyesight.

○ ○ ○ ○ ○
Moving

The invisible girl moved with the woman and man and their children to another house. The new house was full of excitement and accidents. The ambulance had to take the toddler, the woman and a very large teenage boy to the hospital. The teenage boy had taken the toddler with him, while driving and there was an accident, the toddler had been hurt. The toddler had to wear a helmet after the accident. The woman was sad. One day, the invisible girl was standing on a stool to reach a box of cereal in the cabinets. The invisible girl reached the cereal and while stepping down knocked some other items off the shelf; the item hit the invisible girl in the head. The invisible girl had a knot on her head over the right eye. No one helped the invisible girl or comfort her. The other children in the kitchen room laughed at her. The invisible girl rubbed her knot to comfort herself. The invisible girl moved with the woman and the man and their children to another house. The house was on a narrow street, and the house was a tiny house. Matter of fact all the houses on the street were stuck together, brick by brick we were living in very close quarters on a narrow street in a tiny house.

○ ○ ○ ○ ○
The Fire

One school morning, the invisible girl arose early to prepare herself for school. The invisible girl was now in the fourth year of elementary school. The invisible girl had finished dressing herself. The invisible girl had on a pretty gold striped dress, the dress sparkled, as the beads beat against the shiny fabric. Someone had given the invisible girl that dress. The invisible girl decided to wear that dress to school. This was a special day at school. The invisible girl had on black shiny shoes, white ankle socks and her sparkling beaded shiny fabric golden dress, and a cream color thin sweater.

The invisible girl had decided to give her hair a warm press. The woman in the house had warm pressed the invisible girl hair and had showed her how to warm press her hair. The invisible girl had warm pressed her hair before, the woman had taught her how to care for herself. The invisible girl had watched the woman warm press the other girls in the house hair with a straightening comb. The invisible girl decided to warm press her hair, the invisible girl always had favorite her hair in a certain style. The hairstyle was a pixie style. The invisible girl hair was not very long; the invisible girl hair was short and neatly grown. The invisible girl managed her hair style for some time now.

 The invisible girl went downstairs to the small kitchen in the tiny house. The invisible girl noticed that the large teenage boy was lying on the couch. The large teenage boy was home from a juvenile center. The large teenage boy hand was dangling from the couch as he lay upon the couch. He said. "Hi", and told the invisible girl his name and that he was home forever now. The woman and the man living in the house was still asleep upstairs in the house, as well as the other children. But the invisible girl did hear some noise, so she thought to herself, that they are about to get up. Therefore, the invisible girl wanted to hurry. The invisible girl did not want to be in the kitchen when the woman, the man, and the other children came downstairs. See the invisible girl always made a habit of getting up early to prepare for school. And this day she did not want to make it an exception, just because the large teenage boy was home from juvenile.

The invisible girl went into the kitchen to turn on the stove. She asked, the large teenage boy for some matches to light one of the burners. The invisible girl uses the matches to light the burner. She gave the matches back to the large teenage boy lying on the couch. The large teenage boy began to talk with the invisible girl. The large teenage boy told the invisible girl that while in juvenile, some firemen came to talk to the juvenile center to teach fire safety. The invisible girl told the large teenage boy that she did not have time to talk anymore because she had to warm press her hair. But, the large teenage boy insisted that she listen, the large teenage boy told the invisible girl that the fire men taught him how to save someone in case there was a fire. The large teenage boy explained that a person can be rolled in carpet or a blanket to put out the fire. The large teenage boy began to demonstrate how it was to be performed, but the invisible girl said, "No", she did not have time to do that. Because, the invisible girl had to warm comb her hair. The large teenage boy was angry and lay back down on the couch. The large teenage boy had just come out of juvenile.

The invisible girl went into the small kitchen which was not far from the living room where the large teenage boy lay on the couch. The invisible girl grabbed the straightening comb and placed it on the fire. The invisible girl did not leave it there very long, just warm enough to warm press her hair. The invisible girl took the warm comb off the burner and became pressing one side of her hair. Next, she placed the straightening comb back on the fire. The large teenage boy said something to her but she did not respond; the invisible girl did not want to lose focus of what she was doing. The invisible girl notices that she had left the straightening comb on the fire too long. So, she set the straightening comb on the side of the stove to cool off.

The invisible girl went into the living room to see what the large teenage boy wanted. But when she went to the couch she noticed that the large teenage boy eyes were close. The invisible girl called out his name but the large teenage boy said nothing. The invisible girl went back to the kitchen; the straightening comb had cooled off. The invisible girl started pressing the other side of her hair. The invisible girl felt as if someone was behind her as she straightens her hair. The invisible girl kept turning around to look behind herself but there was no one there. The invisible girl continued to warm comb her hair.

While warm combing her hair, the invisible girl noticed that the end of her sweater was dangling over the fire as the invisible girl stood near the burner The invisible girl raised her right arm higher so not to let the ends of the sweater to touch the fire as she turned the burner down. The invisible girl heard some slight noise but thought to herself it must be the large teenage boy moving around on the couch. The invisible girl did not turn around to see, if the large teenage boy was still on the couch. As, the invisible girl put the final touches on her hair, she laid the straightening comb on the side of the burner. The invisible girl looked down and around and noticed that the back of the bottom of her sparkling beaded shiny golden striped dress was on fire.

The invisible girl began to turn around and around patting herself to put out the fire. The invisible girl ran into the living room where the large teenage boy was lying on the couch. The invisible girl cried out for help and the large teenage boy jumped up and yelled to the man and woman upstairs that the invisible girl was on fire. The large teenage boy put the invisible girl on the rub that was near the couch and rolled the invisible girl in the rug to put out the fire. The fire was put out. The invisible girl said to the large teenage boy, "How could this have happen, you set me on fire; just to show how you can put a fire out". The large teenage boy laughed and said." No, I did not you should not be straightening your hair near the fire" He told the man and woman who had ran downstairs what had happened. The large teenage boy was laughing and said to them jumping up and down, "I save her I saved her".

The woman with the large teenage boy took the invisible girl to the emergency room of the hospital. The large teenage boy took the invisible girl in his arms to the hospital. Though the invisible girl wanted to walk, but it had been too painful. The invisible girl had placed ice cubes on the area of the dress that had been burned by the fire, the fire burned the entire back of the dress from front to back and from up to down. The doctors told the woman in the hospital that the invisible girl was a miracle, in spite of the fact that the invisible girl back and buttocks did not burn. The invisible girl suffered burns to the middle area of her left thigh, and the middle of her stomach. And this is how your slave treated me. He burned me through anger. (Genesis 39:19, ESV) and (Ezekiel 22:20, ESV)

○ ○ ○ ○ ○
Out of Elementary School

The remaining of the school year, the invisible girl stayed at home. The school district had the invisible girl's elementary school send home class work; so that the invisible girl to complete her school assignments at home. The invisible girl stayed home the remainder of the year. The invisible girl did her homework and home assignments at home. The invisible girl, teacher and classmates had written the invisible girl a get well card. And each class member signed the card. The card was presented to the invisible girl by the invisible girl class friend. The invisible girl was very happy. The invisible girl was over whelmed with happiness. The invisible girl felt like the teacher, and all class friends and friend really showed that they cared.

○ ○ ○ ○ ○

The Fight

The fight began at recess, but the punches rolled out when the bell rang at the end of the schoolday. The invisible girl was talking with friends doing recess, dodge ball had just ended. The invisible girl was talking with one bigger girl. The invisible girl and some other girls began to sit on the school steps to play jacks and to talk. The bigger girl lived nearby the school in the projects. The invisible girl was telling the bigger girl that she could come over to her house to play jacks. The bigger girl agreed that this would be alright. The bigger girl and a not so big girl always played together doing recess. But, on this particular day one other girl and her friend who was not in the invisible girl class came over and began to talk with the girls. The invisible girl looked at the other girl who appeared to be bossy and pushy as she talked while walking toward the girls. The invisible girl did not want the bossy pushy girl to talk to the bigger girl and her friends, because these were her' friends. The invisible girl felt like she did not need any more girls to talk too.

Suddenly the bossy, pushy girl walked towards the invisible girl and whispered to the invisible girl, "Don't play with them, come and play with us". As she begin, pointing toward herself and the other girl whom she was with. "No", said the invisible girl. "You go away, I do not want to play with you and the other girl". The bossy, pushy girl, began to take the invisible girl by the hand, pulling her away from the bigger girl and her friends. The invisible girl again said, "No, I do not want to play with you". The invisible girl grew angry at the bossy, pushy girl. The bossy, pushy girl again, grabbed hold of the invisible girl and pulled her away. And then, then said, "Do not play with them, they are bad, come with us". The bossy, pushy girl began name calling on the bigger girl. The invisible girl did not like this, and insisted that the bossy, pushy girl go away. Still grabbing and pulling the invisible girl away from the bigger girl in particular. The invisible girl began to pull away from the bossy, pushy girl and pulled her hand away from her. The bossy, pushy girl stepped in front of the invisible girl and said. "Come with us". The invisible girl said again, "No". The bossy, pushy girl began to pull at the invisible girl hand again, and the invisible girl balled up her fist and punched the bossy, pushy girl in the face. Next, the bossy, pushy girl began punching on the invisible girl. The two girls began to push and punch on each other until they both fell on the ground; Punching and tossing one another.

Suddenly the invisible girl teacher pulled both girls apart and told informed both to stop. The bell rang it was time to go home. All the school boys and girls began calling out, "She won, no she won". The teacher told everyone to go home. The invisible girl bigger friend and other friends went home. They were astonished and afraid of the bossy, pushy girl.

After everyone left the invisible girl and the bossy, pushy girl became to fuss at one another. The invisible girl told the bossy, pushy girl that she does not have to play with her if she did not want to. The bossy, pushy girl and the other girl said, "You should play with us, and not that bigger girl because she's bad". They yelled back and forth; the bossy, pushy girl and the invisible girl began to hit on each other and then they both fell on the ground again and began to punch on one another. Then a member of the bossy, pushy girl family came up to stop the fight. They said. "No go on and fight". The bossy, pushy girl and the invisible girl began to fight again. The bossy, pushy girl was on top of the invisible girl punching her while the invisible girl was pulling on the hair of the bossy, pushy girl. The bossy pushy girl arms were around the invisible girl neck; next the invisible girl arms were around the bossy, pushy girl neck. The girls both were intertwined together. Then one of the bossy, pushy girl family members said, "Get up".

When the bossy, pushy girl got up off the invisible girl and both necks were released; the invisible girl blouse flew open. "Oh my goodness, irk, ill, what is that". The invisible girl's scar from her burn doing the fire was showing. The invisible girl got up embarrassed to see that the bossy pushy girl had seen. No one but the invisible girl doctor, mother, sisters and brothers and one friend had seen the burn scar. Now, it had felt like the entire world had seen her burn scar.

The invisible girl's sisters who lived sometimes at the man and woman house had come to pick her up from school. The bossy pushy girl one of her family members and the invisible girl's sister began to argue. They argued as if they knew one another. They then walked away. The invisible girl went away with the sister that sometimes stayed with the man and woman at the house.

Finally, one day after school; the invisible girl saw the bossy, pushy girl. The bossy, pushy girl came to her and said."My family has moved, we moved to the projects, and I will not be coming to this school anymore". The invisible girl thought to herself, why is she telling me where she is going, that is very nice of her. "Well good bye, I hope you go to a nice school".

○ ○ ○ ○ ○

The Grocery Store

The man that was sitting in the window, holding the toddler when the big lady brought me to that house: he later had a grocery, deli like, fresh fruits and vegetable store. When I was around eight years old; I came home from elementary school, on some days I had to work behind the counter of the grocery store. I learned to sliced meats, count change, wait on customers, bag grocery items, and give change to customers. The most part I enjoyed the more was waiting on my schoolmates from Edward Epstein School, my school mates would come into the store to purchase candy, and they would always come in packs and rush in with their nickels and pennies. I would always be coached to go over and help them right away to get them out of the store. I do not think the man that owned the store liked kids that much, though he has twelve children himself. Not including myself. The store was always crowded with men, sitting near the window sill of the store drinking coffee, smoking cigars, and cigarettes debating, but seemed like arguing. I really do not know what they were talking about, some of the men were supposed to be my uncles; some were the store owners friends, still others were just passer bys. One day, a particular man came into the store. I was behind the counter that day, he said, "Hello", to me and brought some candy; The man that owned the store knew of him and replied, "Hello" too. Then he replied to the other man that I was someone's great granddaughter. And the other man whom came into the store to purchase candy became very happy of what he had mentioned. Next, he began smiling and then walked out of the store waving goodbye to me as I waved back. I met that same man ten years later. My heart could not take what transcribed then, and my heart was shattered to pieces and it not only touched my psyche but it touched my very soul. I now know when persons say, "some things people need not know", but I reply there are some things that some persons should not SEE because of the kind of heart one may have.

○ ○ ○ ○ ○
At The Funeral

The invisible girl, who is now, 10 years old, attends a funeral. The woman and man with all the children came to the invisible girl one day and said, "You are going to a funeral. Your grandfather has died". The man whom previously would sit staring out the window while holding a baby; has another daughter from another woman and she would be the driver in the car for attending the funeral. The woman got the invisible girl all dressed up that day. The woman wham's son was lying on the couch the day of the fire would be attending the funeral.

The woman and the man argued the day of funeral. The argument was over which of all the children would be attending the funeral. The man said it would be the tall girl. The tall girl, for whom the woman did send searching for the invisible girl; on the invisible girl's first day of school. The woman said. "No", it would have to be the invisible girl. Why, because the woman said. "She's the grandfather's first great-grandchild". The woman and the man finally agreed that it would be the invisible girl and the boy who was lying on the couch on the day of the fire. Though he was not a boy anymore, he was a young man. The man that was sitting by the open window holding the baby, the woman and the boy that was lying on the couch all got into the car. While in the car, the invisible girl knew a little about funerals, it was a time of sadness. The invisible girl became to pretend she was crying. The invisible girl remembered what the big woman had told her when she was younger. The big woman said."Be nice to this family and the children." The invisible girl and the boy sat in the back of the car, the man and woman sat in the front with the man's younger daughter; the driver. While in the car, the invisible girl asked the woman, "Is this your father's funeral?" "No", said the woman. "He is my grandfather and your great-grandfather." Suddenly, the man's daughter looked over at her father and the woman and said "You have not told her yet". The woman and the man both laughed. The boy began to laugh too.

As the car drove into where the funeral was being held; everyone got out of the car. We saw a long line of people walking in a line toward their cars. The man younger daughter said, "We are late". She said, "We are late for the funeral services". While we were walking a lady within the line of people said. Pointing toward me "What is she doing here?" The woman said. "She should be here. She is his first grandchild". Some of the people in the line of people began to get angry.

Suddenly, the invisible girl noticed a little boy dressed up in a suit; they both locked eyes for a moment. Next, the invisible girl said. "Hi" to the little boy. The little boy smiled back at the invisible girl. The woman pulled the invisible girl away and the other people in the line of walking towards their cars pulled the little boy away. Everyone got back in their cars and drove away.

○ ○ ○ ○ ○

The Bedroom

The invisible girl is now thirteen years of age. The invisible girl would always keep the house clean, neat and tidy. The invisible girl would clean the big house from top to bottom. Every room in the house, the invisible girl would clean and make tidy. The house has two bedrooms on the third floor, five bedrooms on the second floor with one bathroom and a bedroom with a wash room and a bathroom on the first floor. The rooms on the floor to the entrance of the house had a living room, dining room, kitchen, laundry room. The invisible girl wanted to keep the man and woman and their children happy by keeping their rooms clean and tidy.

One day the little girl was finishing up cleaning and was finishing up in the room were the man and woman went to bed. The man came into the room. He asked the invisible girl, "What are you doing in this room"; after slamming the door behind himself. He then went on to say, "My brother told me you pulled your dress up in front of him, and showed him your private parts". The invisible girl was scared. She said. "I just was playing; I did not mean any trouble". Suddenly, the man threw the invisible girl on the bed, and said to her, "You are going to do for me what your mother would not do."

The man pulled the invisible girl dress up, the invisible girl screamed out, "no", to the man, "do not do this, this is wrong". The man got up and pulled a gun out from under the mattress, "now", he said. Placing the gun against the invisible girl head, while pulling her dress up further and pulling down her panties. The invisible girl grew frantic, and was pleading with the man not to go any further, while the man was pulling down his zipper and pulling out his private parts He screamed at the invisible girl to put his private parts inside her privates.

The invisible girl was thinking "This is wrong, I got to persuade him not to do this". The man place the invisible girl hand on his private part and told her to put the private part inside of her, the invisible girl did not do what the man screamed at her to do. Instead she placed it between her buttocks and held her butt cheeks together. The invisible girl said, to the man, "it is in", the man began to move up and down, back and forth, on the invisible girl, trying to kiss the invisible girl on the neck and cheeks as the invisible girl tossed and turned away.

This lasted for a few minutes; suddenly the man lifted himself up off the invisible girl and said. "It is not inside of you", "I said put it inside of you or I will blow your brains out"; All while holding the gun to the invisible girl's head. The invisible girl tried again; thinking of how she would try to fool the man holding the gun to her head. The invisible girl was frantic in trying to place it inside of her private area.

The bedroom door flew open. The woman walked in the bedroom. The woman shouted. "What are you doing? Get off of her". The man jumped up off the invisible girl. The man says, to the woman while holding the gun in his hand. "Her mother would not do it with me, so, she can, she is not my child, and you know this". The woman yelled at the invisible girl, "get out of the room , and never come into the bedroom again, and stop cleaning." "You do not have too" The invisible girl ran out of the man and woman bedroom into her bedroom which was across from the man and woman bedroom. Then, the bedroom door slammed shut.

The invisible girl could hear the man and woman arguing. Next, the woman opens the door and came over to the invisible girl bedroom and asked her. "Are you alright?" The invisible girl said, "I was scared. I did not want to do it". Crying she said, "He told me to put it inside; I fooled him and laid it on my buttocks cheeks and squeezed it together". The woman and the invisible girl began to laugh together; the woman said to the invisible girl, "the only room I want you to clean is your room; Do not never go into our bedroom again". And the invisible girl never went back into the man and woman bedroom again.

The invisible girl overheard the man and woman talking "Now look at what you have done, you know what we must do we got to go and tell someone you know who we got to go and tell". The next day the man and woman got up early that day and left together, they did not come home until later that afternoon. When the man and woman came home the invisible girl was sitting on the living room floor watching television. The woman told the invisible girl to turn off the television because the man had something to tell her. The man began weeping fearlessly, the invisible girl had never seen a man cry before tears were streaming down his face as if he was a child. As the tears fell, the man said to the invisible girl "I am sorry for what I did". The invisible girl was overwhelmed with emotion, no one had ever told her that they were sorry before, especially an adult; that is what the invisible girl was thinking. The invisible girl immediately consul the man and told him to "stop crying" and that "he is forgiven" The invisible girl gave the man a hug and told him that "everything would be alright", and not too worry.

Afterthought

When finish reading this book. In retrospect of what has happen to this invisible little girl's life, it is no way that the author of this book is trying to place blame, disassociation or hatred towards anyone living or those whom associate themselves with the deceased. I pray that this book will change hearts toward those who have desires to take advantage of any child or children regardless of whether the child is half siblings, adoptive children, or extended children of families I pray that this book will help those to seek counseling, forgiveness, and therapy and especially get help for any child or children regardless of what age the child or children may be of now.

References

Besharov, D. J. (1994). Responding to child sexual abuse: The need for a balanced approach. In R.E. Behrman (Ed.), the future of children, 3 & 4, 135-155. Los Altos, CA: The Center for the Future of Children, The David and Lucile Packard Foundation.

Bottoms, B., & Epstein, M. (1998). Memories of childhood sexual abuse: A survey of young adults. Child Abuse & Neglect, 22(12), 1217-1238.

U.S. Department of Health and Human Services, Administration on Children, Youth, and Families. (2007). Child maltreatment 2005. Washington, DC: U.S. Government Printing Office

The Holy Bible, English Standard Copyright © 2001 by Crossway Bibles, a division of Good News Publishers.

http://kids.niehs.nih.gov/lyrics/green.htm

About the Author

Margie Garris is a radio web show host of First Bible Reading on Blogtalkradio. com. And this is a place where Margie shares her personal journey through life ups and downs all while glorifying Christ in the journey. She is also the leading prayer host for First Bible Reading Prayer Call -In This is a place to which everyone may join her prayer line at TalkShoeCommunity.com

Ms. Garris is a 2010 graduate of University of Phoenix. And when, she isn't trying to finish up her graduate studies, in teaching, you may find her volunteering her services and tutoring beginning and comprehensive readers at a local community literacy reading program. When Margie has spare time, she enjoys knitting, cooking and running. She may be contacted at firstbiblereadin1@gmail.com

Printed in the United States
By Bookmasters